Prologue

My name is Jowell Travis Le Gendre and I was born on October 17, 1988, in King's County Hospital in Brooklyn, New York. Today's date is November 22, 2021. Last month on the 17th, I turned 33.

On September 19, 2018, I was arrested for forcible sodomy, object sexual penetration, robbery, and credit card theft in Charlottesville, Virginia. All four charges were alleged by Naomi Gaba, then a student at the University of Virginia.

A little over a year later, on November 8, 2019, in the Circuit Court for the City of Charlottesville, I was convicted of the charges above. A few months later, I was sentenced in February of 2020.

Tonight I am laying on a "mattress" in segregation at Keen Mountain Correctional Center (listening to Lifetime by Maxwell) with a release date in 2060.

Everything you are about to read can be verified through the official court transcripts for all related hearings or through minimal research. It will not be doctored or proofed for errors or eloquence. How I feel is how I will type it. I possess more than enough education to create something comprehensible. That is my goal. I priced it as cheap as I could on Amazon. If I do make any kind of money from this it will go first, to helping my mother. Second, to my legal fight.

At the end of this, all court dates and reference checkpoints will be listed. As far as I know things such as the court transcripts is public information, so anyone should be able to review it. However, if you wish to read these documents yourself and are meeting obstruction, I have them all and I would gladly make copies. Feel free to contact me via email, prison email, or USPS. All contact information can be found at the end of the accounting.

The Truth, Yet I'm Not Free

Chapter 1

The beginning of the events seems like the best place to begin. The where would be on the grounds of the University of Virginia. One of the well-known truths of society which we collectively and willingly overlook is the illegal drug usage in postsecondary education. Some of it is recreational. Some of it comes from peer pressure. Believe it or not, some of it is actually consumed to help cope with depression, anxiety, loneliness, or one of the other mental struggles people quietly face every day.

Quite a few students turn to medications, like Adderall, to stay up and study or to focus.

It is a delusion. It justifies prescription drugs, which justifies narcotics (such as cocaine) used for educational reasons, which justifies recreational.

This is a problem that too many, me included, have exploited for profit. This is a situation where no one can point a finger. We are all responsible. The users, the dealers, the enablers, and the blissfully blind. The drug leads to many more victims besides the user.

Just as I willingly accepted my share of the wrong, I demand my share of the wronged.

"Front." This is a term used in the drug circle which means to give up some type of merchandise but not collecting payment until a later date. There are many errors in this practice. It is an unwritten rule among dealers that you NEVER "front" more than you can stand to lose. Why? Because when something goes wrong, it's not just a little of profit you piss away and "charge to the game." Now its rent. Now its a phone bill. Now its money you borrowed yourself.

Introducing the accuser of the wrongs, Naomi Gaba. Naomi was a grad student at UVA when I met her. Naomi spent a few hundred dollars on prescription pills and cocaine. MDMA once but it wasn't her thing. When Naomi asked for some merchandise on consignment, no alarms went off. When I didn't hear from her by the agreed update, still no red flags. When I tried to reach her and couldn't, I was a little worried.

See I broke, the rule about not fronting more than I could stand to lose. Overconfidence in the fast drug money led me to care less and less about my little gas station job. I was spending like there was no tomorrow. And I had to get my weed.

Well, poetically enough, right around the time I stopped caring enough to quit my job, the individual I purchased merchandise to disperse decided to flex his muscles a bit. I went and found a new distribution center. Turned out to be better prices worse product. I was green. I admit that I was inexperienced with most drugs. No one who can say this so candidly should be in the business. At the time, a close city had some stuff coming out that looked like sparkly snowballs when you cracked them open. Fishscales. In my naive mind, I thought a struck gold. By the time I figured out that I was wrong, it was too late to fix. I could no longer afford any losses. The money Naomi owed me, pre fishscales, needed to be recovered asap.

I finally got a hold of the young lady. We agreed to meet one of the streets that had some off campus housing for students. 14th Street. There wasn't tension but I was high strung by this point. State of emergency. Now I was the one ducking phone calls. Had I just called and been like "Yo, I fucked up." everything could be different right now. I took the cowardly prideful route.

When we stopped to talk, I skipped the necessities. I needed the few bills I was looking for. My Muslim cellmate has to stop saying that he knew something before it occurred because it puts too much of an omniscient aura around man that should be reserved for god. With all due respect to whoever's beliefs, I knew.

She had the money but she wanted more on consignment. She needed to get to the ATM. I wanted to collect and dip out. I was dry. I had a couple more grams of the b.s. product on me earlier but that sale happened minutes ago, right up the street on Wertland, and they had cash then and there. I couldn't sell her a Tylenol because I couldn't spare the money to buy the bottle. Of course, I knew that if I told her that then and there, the odds of me getting my money from this white girl would evaporate. That's when I got creative.

What I had on me was already spoken for, but I was gonna go meet my plug after her (I had nothing at all, then or later on that night). He's not answering his phone. I got you just let me get my bread.

Finally I was like, give me mines and I will come back through later. She wanted to pay me later when I came back through. She even suggested me holding a card. My problem was that I had no intention of coming back. After a couple volleys back and forth, she asked for my dealers number. I just knew that I was good when I gave her the bullshit number

What I didn't expect was for the little bitch to text right then and there. She said that as soon as my peoples responded, she would take care of me. I got tired of waiting. I told her so, then exit stage right. Naomi wasn't going for it.

Now words were being exchanged with some heat. Very little physical at that point. Some grabbing my arm and whatnot. That all changed when she went into her book bag.

I know how hard it will be to believe but this tiny anorexic college white chick came at me, a decent sized black male, with a knife and slashed me on the arm.

Not once throughout the trial, the lawyers and the cops have I denied this next part: I punched her in her mouth. Hard. I don't regret it. I honestly wish I'd hit her harder. Enough to make forty odd years of my time worth it, harder. One of her teeth was knocked back and ended up "dying" I wish I had knocked out her front four top and bottom so that she would think of me every time she looked in the mirror. That might've made the forty worthwhile.

Naomi went for her bag again so I followed. She pulled out a knife the first time. There was no telling what else was in there. I snatched, slung it, then got missing. I didn't run but I wasn't taking a leisurely stroll either. I just wanted to get away from a potential news headliner.

Did it anyway. Go figure.

That's all that took place between Naomi and myself that night. By the time news was on the next morning, a picture of my face in the red T-shirt I had on was on the news saying that I was wanted in investigation of a sexual assault.

The Truth, Yet I'm Not Free

Chapter2

I was arrested and transported to Albemarle Charlottesville Regional Jail after I was interviewed and question by police.

In the upcoming days or weeks, I was assigned JD Beard, of the public defender's office, as my attorney. Mr. Beard was the first person to tell me that no one was going to believe that the little bitch attacked me. And she was screaming rape.

My lawyer and I met and spoke on several occasions. He was very good about communicating and responding to my messages promptly. I ended up asking him to put in a motion to withdraw as counsel because I felt that all he wanted to do was talk about guilty pleas. I think that he started with a floor of 40 years will no ceiling.

When JD Beard was replaced, it was with Holly Vrandenburg. Ms. Vrandenburgh and I got along decent. My mother and older sister were behind me every step of the way. If I couldn't get a hold of my attorney, they were more than happy to help. I think that she didn't like that but I was fighting for my life and they were too.

A few months after she was appointed counsel, my preliminary hearing came up. There are very few things that we defendants have complete say so about in the criminal legislation process, prelims is one of them. There are a few defensive purposes for the preliminary hearing. The main one I wanted to utilize was getting some of the witnesses testimony scratched in stone, as I informed my attorney.

Any staff member at Albemarle Charlottesville Regional Jail can verified the amount of time I put in on the law library computer. When Ms. Vrandenburgh told me that we wouldn't get a chance to cross examine because the Commonwealth wouldn't put her on the stand I, knowing that a witness on the stand belongs neither to the prosecution or the defense, suggested putting her up as our own so that we could direct examine her and let the Commonwealth worry about the cross. This she refused. In the holding cell of the courthouse, Ms. Vrandenburgh told me that she did not agree with that course of action and that if I followed that course she would cooperate.

I did as she suggested. The moment I got back to the jail I wrote a letter to Ms. Vrandenburgh replaying our conversation in the holding area. I put in her refusal to actively participate in a preliminary hearing. I sent a copy to her and copy to the Court to be placed in file in case it be needed later on.

In response to this letter Ms. Vrandenburgh promptly responded with a letter saying that she wanted me to write another letter recanting all that was said in the first. Her letter said that if I didn't comply, she would withdraw as counsel. I still have the original with her letter head and signature.

Just like JD Beard, Holly Vradenburg filed a motion to withdraw as counsel, which she was granted. Unlike JD Beard, I didn't ask miss Vrandenburgh to withdraw. She even went as far as to say that she had to contact some type off bar hotline for advice before she came to her decision. She also said that the prosecution asked her to think of the victim. She chose the victim's comfort over my case. The July 9, 2019, transcript will verify this.

Later on I will quote a judge accusing me giving Ms. Vrandenburgh a hard time but clearly says that is not the issue. She goes as far as to say that she likes me. I will go into more detail later on.

Please check the reference in the back of this book for the exact hearing dates, pages and lines if you wish to fact check my claims. I promise to at least do better than our previous leader did on social media.

It just occurred to me that Judge Moore said that he would personally call the list of lawyers he had. I'm not sure if that violative of the law or my rights but I will definitely be looking into it. Might be useful in my Habeus Corpus.

The next attorney to represent me was Anthony Martin. I would like to point out several things before I truly begin this story. 1) Martin was my third attorney. 2) At the time, ten months of incarceration, I had not yet been arraigned. I had not yet given indication of whether I would take a jury or bench trial. 3)Mr. Martin was on vacation the first two weeks as my attorney. "Representation" didn't begin until the month of August. 4)A hearing took place without me or my attorney on 6/17/19 being present. I didn't even know of the hearing or that shit like it was legal. Dates, time needed to hear the case and whether it would be judge or jury was determined without my knowledge, input or consent. I found out about 6/17/19 post conviction. I didn't choose whether I wanted a jury or bench trial until 10/29/19. I will get to 10/29/19, first we must discuss 10/3/19.

By the time I met Mr. Martin, I was in the habit of sending copies of all correspondence with attorneys to be preserved in my court file. With good reason. Mr. Martin and I started off horrible. For one, he contacted after his vacation in August. He felt two to three months was enough time to read everything on the case, formulate a plan, arrange evidence and witnesses, and execute a decent defense. Of course, he eventually made it clear that he didn't believe that I was innocent, so such things wouldn't matter. He did not insinuate the fact. Nor did he hint at it. Mr. Martin blatantly told me that he was not going to waste time on evidence and a detailed defense when we both knew that I was guilty. His words, not mine.

He even got an attitude when I informed him that I was never arraigned and that I had never waived my right to a jury trial. "I don't like being jerked around," were his exact words.

That was the most upset I have ever felt in my life. No that was the most violently upset I had ever been in my life. Nothing came close. I wanted to knock out Naomi's starting line up for starting all this. I wanted this scrawny, ignorant, under qualified, fraternizing, pussy to have a whole new set. I wanted him to have surgery. He alone justified every ass whooping attorneys have ever taken at the hand of an unsatisfied criminal defense client. I'm not saying they all deserved it. I'm saying that clowns like him made it hard for people like you. If there could have been a type of messianic, sacrificial attorney to take all of the abuse lawyers would face in the future, I am behind him with my size twelves giving him all of the encouragement he would need. I remained polite. No threats in the courtroom. I knew that they wanted a monster so I refused to give it to them.

Of course, I immediately asked him to put in a motion to withdraw as counsel. This brings us to the memorial October 3, 2019.

When I walked into the court room I noticed that it wasn't the right judge. This, I later found out, was judge Franklin. I walked onto a stage and I was the only one who had not previously reviewed the script.

The purpose of the hearing was to address the motion I had asked my attorney to submit. Mr. Martin informed the court that I do not trust him and that I do not have faith in his abilities.

Page 6 and 7 of the transcript for the 10/3/19 hearing is dominated by Joseph Platania putting Ms. Vradenburgh's withdrawal before the court as if it were at my request. He said that it was a communication issue when my attorney had just told them that I did not trust him and that I had no faith in his abilities. Mr. Martin refused to get the transcripts so I was unable to challenge Mr. Platania when he manipulated the record by citing me asking for another attorney without mentioning that I clearly stated that I was not asking for Ms. Vradenburgh's withdrawal but if she was replaced I would need representation.

I anticipated something similar so I had the letter in which she clearly stated that it was her decision but Mr. Martin would not present the letter.

It was decided that appointing me new counsel would, by necessity, call for a continuance so that the next attorney would have adequate time to prepare. This would prove to be a major inconvenience to witnesses and such, even though the law says that a defendant's rights trump the inconvenience of witnesses. In the end, I was given the option of representing myself while facing three life sentences or keep the man who had already convicted me in his head because the judge said that I had abused my right to legal counsel.

I kept him, making a promise to myself to do everything possible to record evidence of his treachery. Starting then and there.

I asked judge Franklin if everything was recorded. When he said that they were, I asked that it be noted that "I'm keeping Mr. Martin as my counsel, but even to this matter, I gave him a letter to ask him to present to the judge and present to the court and he still refused that. But I will keep as counsel." That is me quoting myself from the transcript. Please forgive the poor speech. I was a little pissed off.

When franklin attempted to downplay the situation, I took the opportunity to leave evidence of Mr. Martin's comments outside the courtroom. "Its hard for me to trust an attorney that doesn't, you can't--- you can't come to court believing that client's guilty and then try to tell a jury of twelve he's innocent."

It wasn't until months later that I found out, through research done by my mother or older sister, that anytime an attorney refused a course of action because he knew that their client was guilty, was automatically considered ineffective assistance of counsel. I cried when I read that because I knew that I learned it too late. I cried hard. I tried to tell a judge, smh, later for that.

A few weeks later on 10/29/19, a week before trial was to begin, we were in front of the regular judge Moore. My attorney had finally decided to request an expert witness. It was denied, of course.

I was arraigned, one week before trial. Mr. Martin didn't even discuss the fact that I was about to be arraigned. They (my attorney, the prosecutor and the judge) discussed it then an there. "This date would work", "no I can't do it then". Finally, the Commonwealth was like hey, let's do it now. We didn't go into the back and discuss the pros and cons. He just leaned over (his breath was always foul. He kept stealing the Jolly Ranchers my sister bought me from commissary at trial) and told me to plead not guilty. The idiot was even dumb enough to repeat it out loud so that it could be saved on the record. I probably could have argued for some kind of redo since I was never given the explanation of a guilty plea or an Alford plea. Hindsight... And Habeus Corpus.

Nobody, myself included thought to point out the fact that it was impossible for them to have come to a decision about whether I wanted a bench trial or jury trial (referring to my desire for a jury being a stall tactic) since we didn't even know if I was to plead guilty or not guilty. Hell, I didn't learn details and benefits of an Alford plea until later.

This will not be the only time validation of my claims come out but too late to change the perception of my character in the court of law.

At this point I wish to highlight a couple of things for future reference. 1)I kept Mr. Martin because the prosecution and Judge Franklin said that the Commonwealth did it's part in giving me fair assistance of counsel and that it was at my request that Holly Vradenburgh was removed. 2)They told me it was either him or no one. 3)The fact that I "changed my mind" about proceeding with a bench trial as a stall tactic weighed in on the denial and that was bullshit as stated above. No telling how things would have looked had it been pointed out that I didn't request Ms. Vradenburgh's removal and that I never chose a bench trial. Then again, if it was all a circus act, there wasn't anything I could've done but leave a trail of breadcrumbs to be followed later on. I definitely tried.

Chapter3

September 6, 2019. The first day of trial. The courtroom was stuffed beyond maximum capacity. Majority of those present would be excused once jury selection was completed. I read quite a few John Grisham books over the years. Even though it is fiction, the man obviously has a wealth knowledge where the litigation process is involved. I always thought the process of choosing jury members would involve communication between defense attorney and the accused. If so, my experience was abnormal beyond reason. I ate a lot of Jolly Ranchers during that phase.

The part of the jury selection that always stuck with me was when Judge Moore called the jury back in only to dismiss them immediately because he had forgotten something. "...parties agree I don't need to go through a full colloquy again because we've already done the arraignment and I've done that". I know colloquy, it was one of the SAT words I studied a couple decades ago. I had no idea what was left out though. When I asked Mr. Martin, he waved it off as legal jargon. To this day I don't know what it means but I will list it as an error in my Habeus. What Judge Moore said on the following page got my attention, it didn't register the day of. "...but I still had to ask those questions when we're about to start."

Considering that my arraignment, about a week ago, was a rushed and an unorthodox affair, I have to wonder if cutting corners was violative of my due process rights.

Outside of asking my opinion, I had very little to complain about. I think that I got off lucky when a Ms. Haney sent a message to the judge saying that she shouldn't sit on the jury. Mr. Martin motion to strike her without using one of our four but the judge denied the motion. He did offer the opportunity to call the juror in and question her further but he said no. I don't how the judge didn't see it as infringement of my rights but the lady said that she emails both Mr. Platania and Ms. Pather regularly for work reasons. The prosecution said that he thought she was a man(because of the name) and I guess the judge solved it. She also had regular communications with the officers but it was all okay.

The one that did slip through, motions and defensive strikes, was a Mr. Buppert. He said that he knew Mr. Platania socially. He might have said that their kids hang out but I'm not looking for it, so don't quote me. Mr. Platania didn't try to explain it. My lawyer and the judge were okay with it so "Goooo! Tigers!"

I didn't appreciate how he responded to one of the potential replacements in the back who couldn't him. When they asked him to repeat what he had said, he snapped back waspishly telling the woman that he was only speaking to the chosen 21. Judge Moore stepped in diplomatically, letting my attorney know that he needed to speak up without embarrassing anyone. I thought the number one rule in a jury trial was to not piss off the jurors. Even those unchosen. Haven't we learned harming one person in society, more often than not, draws majority of that race and class to their banner?

He did a couple of times with one of the professional witnesses. As an individual with a hard to pronounce name, I make an effort to pronounce others properly. He kept saying Ayob Ayoub. I felt like it was intentional. Small things.

Opening arguments. One of the major drawbacks as being the defendant in a courtroom, aside from the obvious, the prosecution gets to go first. They get to present whatever it is first. When the defense has their say they are faced with being efficient and long winded versus being mercifully brief and sacrificing the meat of their defense.

Mr. Martin didn't have that issue. He didn't prepare a defense. I believe I had more notes prepared than he did. The folder he carried was filled warrants, motions the Commonwealth filed and letters I wrote. I know I definitely took more notes than he did. I wrote questions, made requests for questions I wanted him to ask, and I put huge dark stars next to things that could have been vital even if it was only for me to use post-conviction. He ignored me. Once in a while he would look at the yellow note pad I commandeered. A lot during the prosecution's first witness. Naomi Gaba, the alleged victim.

A couple of highlights from the Commonwealth's opening. Ms. Pather described the alleged victim as hysterical. Ms. Pather told everyone that when Naomi called 911, she said that she was assaulted and robbed. Ms. Pather said that I demanded, and received, oral sex from her bloodied mouth yet I did not rape her because I didn't have a condom. Ms. Pather also mentions my blood being on her without saying how it got there.

I honestly thought that the first day of trial went better than expected, no thanks to Mr. Martin. His parody of a cross examination was comical, as intended, I believe. On their own, the prosecution and the witness set up several opportunities for us to expose the lies. The first trip through questioning, Naomi said that she was struck from the side yet it was a laceration to the front of her mouth and it was a front tooth that was knocked out of place. She was knocked to the ground, thrown to the ground or she fell yet towards the end of her testimony she refused to get on the ground because she feared being raped. She had cuts all over her knees and legs but only her knees touched the ground.

On page 208, she describes herself as in shock but still "focused on survival and kind of just getting out of this situation." Understandable and plausible. A few lines down, she describes herself as hysterical. Hysteria, according to my recollection, occurs in situations on unmanageable... ness? Webster gives me two definitions. 1) a nervous disorder marked esp. by defective emotional control, 2) unmanageable fear or outburst of emotion. I think that "unmanageable" and "defective" would make focusing on survival, or anything for that matter, just a tad bit difficult. But hey, what do I know? I am just another ignorant sex offender.

In her opening statements, Ms. Pather said that Naomi was going to get on the stand and say that she was forced to perform oral sex while bleeding out of the mouth but she was not raped due to lack of condom. As promised, Naomi delivered. She also went on to say that I went through her things. She says that I asked her if she used her headphones and, when she said that she does I put them back. Apparently I also did not take her laptop because she was a student. I am not going to bother looking up the word "robbery" in my dictionary. I will point out two things.

First, and this said with 100% honesty. I am not the oral sex guy. No woman I have ever dealt with would say otherwise. In my opinion, that should have made people from my past go "Oh nah, that bitch is lying." Not to be crass or vulgar but I have NEVER...climaxed from oral sex. Not the kind of guy who gets full off of appetizers. Never has been my kind of thing. This would be like someone telling you I stole that car and went joyriding for a few days. I have maybe driven a total of ten miles in my life and that is including parking lot maneuvering. Actually, majority of it is parking lot maneuvering.

Second, anyone who has ever been a college student or knows anything about the subject knows what am about to say. 9 time out of 10, the most expensive items on a student going to or coming from class or the library are their textbooks and laptop. This young bitch said that she was robbed but the robber was kind enough to leave her headphones because she used them and her laptop because she was a student. Am I the only person who sees some incongruity here?

Ironically, the one item that was "missing" was her cellphone. An iPhone at that. I worked in John Paul Jones Arena some time back (good people to work around). One time I found an iPhone. I called the number and, with some friends, I arranged a meeting with the guy at a bar. I gave him the phone and he offered to buy beers. We talked and I found out that not only could he have remote operated the phone to turn it on and track it from wherever he was, he could have activated some kind of alarm that would have made a rape whistle sound like a whisper. Bad pun?

Well, the alleged victim said that her phone was taken, her iPhone was taken, yet they made no effort to track or retrieve it. What would have been on the phone but there was never an attempt to locate the phone in a situation where a man accused of sexual assault and robbery says that the meeting was prearranged and that it wasn't the first time we met.

I'm trying to be as chronological as I can, in regard to her testimony but it's hard. The device on which I am typing is not exactly equipped for the task so I apologize for being too lazy to go two emails back so I could rearrange minor details. Bear with me.

Along with the forced oral sex, the alleged victim says that she was subjected forced penetration. She actually said an entire finger was inserted into her vagina. A medical examiner is going to, later on, testify that there was no damage to the inside or outside of her canal. She will also say that her hymen was intact. If I am wrong I apologize but I took that as meaning that she was a virgin. I am not an expert on the subject. Virgins aren't really my thing either, no offense.

I understand the anatomy of men varies with each individual. My hands and fingers are not exactly small. I would wager anything that there are penises smaller than my finger, both in length and diameter. I would also bet that those penises, if inserted into a vagina with an unbroken hymen, would tear the "fold of mucous membrane partly closing the opening (oxymoron) of the vagina." Under this assumption, I figured that it would be hard to believe that my finger (joints, nail, knuckle, and all) could enter a virgin's vagina without leaving evidence of its passage. I may be wrong but I am 235 pounds, I have never been a small man. My hands match my body.

Ms. Pather goes on to question the witness about positioning, she said that she was kneeling. Ms. Pather said how, Naomi says she doesn't understand the question. Then she says she doesn't remember. She says I told her to get on the ground after I drug her around the house. Earlier, she said that she refused to get on the ground because she feared being raped, now she is on her knees. Later on she will go on to say that she got on her hands and knees. She was helpless and vulnerable as she was beaten and robbed yet she walked away with her laptop, electronic accessories, schoolbooks (possibly), her life, and her maidenhead? I think the Commonwealth of Virginia should review their definition of robbery and sexual assault.

She finally makes it home, goes through the back door and finds one of her roommates in the kitchen. "I don't remember exactly what I said but something along the lines of I've been, I was just robbed, and I asked if I could borrow her phone to call 911."

It is plausible to consider that she merely forgot to mention that she was sexually assaulted in the heat of the moment. Highly unlucky, in my unlearned opinion but possible. The problem is that she finally offers consistency.

When she first entered the house, according to her first recounting on the stand, she just said that she was robbed and asked to use her roommates phone to call the cops. They played the 911 call and she said that she was robbed. The call from dispatch to officers in the area came out as a robbery. Not a rape or a sexual assault, just a robbery. If sexual assault would have been mentioned, that would have been how dispatched relayed it. Later on, the prosecution will show the initial interview from an officer's body cam. Not once did she mention being sexual assaulted in ANY WAY. None whatsoever. No oral, no penetration of the vagina by a finger or anything else. This could be seen as an oversight. Three times? It's not an oversight, it's an afterthought. As in, "Oh, this will really fix his ass."

My pen was scribbling like crazy at that point but Mr. Martin was oblivious to me. He tells me during a recess that she mentioned it at a later interview that prosecution did not have to show. One thing he did do, and I firmly believe it was unintentional, he got her to say that I came at her from bushes lining the sidewalk (at first she couldn't remember) and he got her to say on the stand that she never fought me, never injured me in anyway.

If that was true, why was my blood on the scene?

Chapter4

I am going to try for some transparency. I'm already convicted with more time than black male life expectancy statistics say I can serve. I've already said it on the stand anyway. This is a thin line I was trying to tightrope. I didn't deny using a credit that didn't belong to me. I was charged with credit card theft, not illegal use or fraud. I didn't take it or beat somebody up for it. It was supposed to be insurance. A deposit to be returned upon fulfillment of promised deeds. Put a hole in your apartment wall then try to get your deposit back. Break the coffee pot in the hotel.

Now, my mind at the time of all of this said that she owed me money. It said, if you owe me money than there can be nothing illegal about me spending my money if its used the same way a normal law abiding American citizens would use it. I didn't go buy drugs (not even weed), I didn't go buy liquor and beer or go out partying. I treated it as if it was the first check of the month (and I was responsible).

I acknowledge that I can't go around confiscating people's shit because I wasn't seeing my bread but, and some people won't like this, banks do it. As do car dealerships, landlords, tax collectors, IRS, social service. Its called repossession, eviction, child support, and any pass you get if you're a big time corporate giant led by people who already made it as opposed to peasants or serfs trying to get by. The crazy part, not too long ago, it was acceptable for them to do worse. Beat you, drag you out of their(your) house in front of your kids and take all of your belongings. To this day, it's okay in some ways. I know you still get harassing calls although that is supposed to be illegal to. They have fucking television shows about it. Anything from a bullshit car you owe a couple thousand on all the way to a yacht or a Cessna. Look for the shows. I dare you. They end up fighting on the shows, people shot and stabbed. They stop people from jumping back into their cars or running back into their house or trailer. On cable networks it's called entertainment if I do it, it's a crime. Next time you see someone preventing someone from going into their house, car, or boat know that you're watching abduction. Check your state laws. If I prevent from going anywhere or force to go this way or that, I have committed abduction.

I am not trying to justify my actions but if ten people are in a room, I block the door and say nobody is leaving til I say so, I get ten counts of abduction.

I have called the cops on somebody twice in my life. Both times it was on the cops. One put his foot in the door not letting me close it. The other, they moved surveillance cameras at a friend's (once upon a time) house then walked in. Rules and laws don't apply to them.

There is a purpose to this section other than ranting and raving at the system. My charges were forcible sodomy (forcing someone to perform oral sex), object sexual penetration(entering a body cavity for sexual purposes without consent), robbery, and credit card theft.

As you just read, I used the credit card. I don't feel that I took it but I will readily admit that she didn't say go get even. Again, I have never okayed the court to take 25% of my paychecks for fines. The prosecution put on a parade of witnesses and professional experts (individuals who received paid days off to testify in favor of the highest bidder). The only evidence presented to support a sexual assault of any kind was the alleged victims testimony. Medical personnel who did the rape kit said no damage at all to the vaginal area. No sperm, skin cells, saliva or hair.

The only DNA evidence (my blood and hers) supported my version of things and contradicted hers since she said that she didn't injure me in anyway. Again, how the fuck did my blood get outside of my skin?

At the most, the evidence presented for next two days verified that both of us bled. That's it, and they proved credit card fraud. At the most.

The only reason I am not granting credit to a robbery is because of her testimony. The problem here is credibility. If my blood is on the scene, yet the accuser's tale doesn't fit, we move into questions of credibility. If an individual gets on the stand lies about one portion of the events that transpired, how can you accept anymore of her testimony?

Actually, in the Commonwealth of Virginia, you can't. Its called perjury. Once a person has committed perjury the stand they are tainted. If they are charged and convicted, they cannot hold certain positions. They can never sit on a jury.

In the Commonwealth of Virginia, you are allowed to respond violently if you fear for the safety of yourself, another, and in a few cases your property. I do not care how big or small you are. If you cut me once, you are a threat. I struck her once and it was in response to being cut.

Cops are putting people six feet deep for drawing a cellphone. I watched a news clip where a school resource officer snatch a fifth grade girl from her desk and slammed her into the floor.

I learned long ago that civil rights movements do reach incarcerated men. If people knew the hardships people face in here. Smh. In the prison I am in alone. Keen Mountain Correctional Center. Black lives matter? One of my goals to accomplish before I die, whether it be in orison or out, is to start a nonprofit organization that covers all of the taboo areas people are scared of.

He Too, for me who were falsely convicted of sex crimes. I understand the risk of fighting to free men who are guilty. Before my organization begins to look into your case, you will sign a contract stating that we will use all relevant material to vindicate, it will also say that condemning evidence will be turned over to prosecution. The multifaceted umbrella will be called Vigilante.

Sorry, I got off the subject. Or did I?

So, when I was first arrested, I am 99% sure that I said I was innocent. Its like the basic rule. With lawyers and at trial, I owned mine. Their evidence, cops, medics, surveillance, and friends supported an illegal use of credit card, an offense which I was not charged with, so I pled not guilty.

Chapter 5

After ruling a defendant guilty, the jury is supposed to recommend a sentence. I am supposed to be present. The deputy that was there convinced the court that it would be in the best interest of everybody involved if I were allowed to skip that portion and return to the jail. At trial, you don't wear restraints. They put a electric belt contraption on my leg to encourage good decision making. I took it off. I knew that if I went back in the courtroom, I would damage my chances of post-conviction remedies. Starting with my attorney who presented nothing because he knew that I was guilty. To this day, I still cry if I get mad enough. Some people would think it's funny. I think it's dangerous. It was some time before I found out what they recommended.

The time between the guilty verdict and sentencing on February 10th was somewhat eventful. The Court finally freed me of Mr. Martin. At his request. All of the reasons he used to withdraw from my case were the same ones I presented at the October 3rd hearing. The only difference was that my trial was already sabotaged.

Some things may seem unbelievable. In such cases, I ask for the reader to remember that I am including a list of court transcript reference points. If you cannot or will not contact the courts to inquire after copies, for whatever reason, yet you wish to know more please contact me using the contact information at the end of this book. I will do the best I can to make sure I send either send requested copies, guide you through the steps or find a way to make it all digitally accessible for readers to fact check free of charge. My goal in his is not money. Its exposure and an attempt to earn my retrial.

The purpose of the hearing was to address Mr. Martin's motion to withdraw as counsel. His, mine was denied about four months back. I didn't even know the purpose of the hearing.

The Truth, Yet I'm Not Free

Mr. Martin literally listed every point I raised in October. I didn't trust him. I had no faith in his abilities. I had asked him to record our sessions on more than one occasion.

Mr. Platania, in an effort to deny me counsel, says that the first two withdrew at my request. Of course I attempted to correct that. When the judge asked me directly if I wanted new counsel I told him yes and no but I informed him that I needed to explain the answer. I was not trying to remove Mr. Martin but if he was replaced I would want a replacement. Page 6 of the transcripts shows me trying to make some things clear for the record. Failed attempt.

Mr. Platania finally admits that I was right about Ms. Vradenburgh requesting withdrawal even though he had intentionally manipulated and misquoted court proceedings so that it looked as if I requested her removal. The third page fourth line 4 of the July 9, 2019, shows me saying "I wasn't asking for new counsel." Yet this was the same transcript from which Mr. Platania said I did. Prosecutorial misconduct, considering that the main reason the judge made me keep Mr. Martin was because the Commonwealth said that I had requested removal of the first two.

He attempts the same trick again at this hearing. He intentionally misquotes again. I tried to correct him and the judge aggressively shut me down. "No. Don't interrupt him right now." I mumbled something then Mr. Platania tried to fix himself while still harming me. "Yeah, but---and I think he's right(me). I see his point that Ms. Vradenburgh also was asking to be removed." The problem was that I NEVER asked it. I made sure to state this on record.

A few very important factors occurred at this point:

1)The judge granted Mr. Martin his removal before hearing my testimony. I am officially considered my own attorney at that point. Pro se litigant.

2)As my own lawyer, I was made to represent myself from the stand. I have never seen an attorney do their work from the stand so that the court and the Commonwealth could cross examine them. Cross examination on a defense attorney? But I complied. I knew that 1/28/20 was just one battle in a war for my life.

From the stand I FINALLY had a chance to fix everything about these attorneys on record. Starting from JD Beard to Martin.

There was no personality conflict between JD Beard and I. In fact neither the judge or the prosecution could speak on details of our relationship because we granted the motion without digging. As a courtesy I let them know that I felt he was more concerned with a plea instead of preparing for trial. He wanted me to take a 40 year plea. 40 year, with no cap and I'm innocent.

I corrected all of the prosecution's lies about Ms. Vradenburgh and her motion to withdraw. Again, what I said on that stand can be verified through 7/9/19 transcript. I pointed out Mr. Martin refusing certain questions on cross, evidence that could have helped, him blatantly saying that he wouldn't waste time because he knew I was guilty, pointing out for the jury that Naomi did not mention sexual assault in her first two or three contacts with officers. Actually, she did not mention sexual assault on any the recordings played in court. I brought how he would not present motions when I had evidence for both. I even told the judge that he was wrote g to say that Mr. Martin Never had this kind of trouble. "I'm not the first to complain," I told him. "I researched my attorney. I'm not the first one to complain about this at these levels." "In other areas too. This is not the first place since the nineties. I researched my attorney. I'm not the first one to complaints. about him."

The judge ignorantly accused me of telling my attorneys how to handle my case and why they're wrong. By law a criminal defendant says 1) prelim or no prelim, 2) guilty or not guilty, 3) jury trial or no jury trial, 4) testify or don't testify. They tell us this and leave it at that. There is one more important piece that like to leave out. The defendant, the accused, determines the objective or the goal. It is the lawyer who decides the strategy to get there, with the client's approval. When I respectfully told him that he was wrong, I experienced open hostility.

Page 28 line 4 "---It is true. It is true and you know it's true." I wish I could access actual video and audio. Just to be clear, JD Beard and I parted on good terms. We shook hands and he wished me well. Ms. Vradenburgh on page 20 of the 7/9/19 hearing Ms. Vradenburgh even said she I liked me. I was touched. I was raised with manners. No attorney can say they were disrespected or that I was impolite. The judge made a rude and unjustified accusation that is not supported by the recorded words of any attorney who has represented me.

In the end, the judge's justification for denying me counsel at sentencing (his first justification, gives another similar one at sentencing) was that he didn't think there would be pointless to appoint me counsel and that the law did not call for the court to do pointless acts. Besides, another judge had already ruled so.

When I tried to explain that the last judge made he decision based on the Commonwealth lying and saying that I was running through attorneys like mad Judge Moore's response was "I don't really care why he ruled that." Truth didn't matter. Then he goes on to terminate my direct examination of myself and offer the Commonwealth an opportunity at cross examination.

He was kind enough to allow me to submit my amateur motions (motion for mistrial and motion to set aside verdict) since I was considered pro se the moment he released Mr. Martin but he would not let me present evidence supporting the motions saying, "I don't need to take any other evidence."

When he said that nothing in the motions would be a basis for a mistrial I asked him about the ineffective assistance of counsel. I went further to it on record (as I did in October) that my attorney wouldn't present evidence because he knew that I was guilty.

He says "I do not find that these allegations, in light of he evidence that was heard, is a basis to set aside the jury's verdict."

Translation, no matter what evidence I presented, I was going to be found guilty. He wouldn't even let me present evidence a few moments ago.

I'm not done. He follows up with "First of all, the Commonwealth is not accepting that," Is he speaking for them or was it already discussed outside of my presence? "So I'm going to deny that motion as well."

I even cited some case law my sister had mailed me. From a case titled Johns v. Smith, it says that when counsel refrains from indicated defensive action because he in WS that his client is guilty, the client is deprived of effective counsel. Didn't matter in that courtroom.

I learned a new legal term that day in the Circuit Court For The City of Charlottesville. "Hobson's choice." What I gathered as the Commonwealth and judge talked around me was that my rights were jeopardized no matter which the judge ruled, he would just choose which one was the lesser of two evils. Quote?

Judge speaking "Well, its what they call a Hobson's choice. I mean, are his rights jeopardized more by not having standby counsel and he represents himself, or are they jeopardized more by having an attorney that doesn't know about the case, but at least can sit through the trial?" What part of that seems fair to a defendant?

He made sure to drive the point home that standby counsel would not help me research or present motions. I was told to get it from the rough, in so many words. I remember one of them saying that an attorney would need at least six months to prepare for the sentencing of my case. I had twelve days to prepare for sentencing. Anthony Martin had 90 days to prepare for trial. Four words: Ineffective Assistance Of Counsel.

Chapter 6

The good thing about sentencing is that the worst has been done. I am mentally off balanced enough that I could survive a few decades incarcerated without further significant deterioration. I can submerge myself in various activities, both positive and uplifting, that would occupy my time and accomplish set goals.

The conviction was the painful part. I could probably fill a tub with the tears I have felt pooling up in my ears as I laid in the bed thinking about what the conviction meant. To me more than others but their opinions weighed in. It was inevitable. Not like I reached out to anyone. But just knowing that I would be known as a predator. Most of my associates were women. After being labelled as a predator, the time was nothing. I didn't even blink.

I fought though. I fought hard. On February 10, 2020, I went before the Circuit Court for The City of Charlottesville one last time.

My sentencing hearing. I did a lot of research up to the point. I couldn't go pass a bar exam but I might have been able to scrape by on a couple quizzes or chapter summaries.

I went into the court with a pretty sound foundation to argue violation of the double jeopardy clause of the Fifth Amendment and for known use of perjured testimony.

In Jones v. Commonwealth the court stated that for the double jeopardy clause of the Fifth Amendment, grand larceny is a lesser included offense of robbery only when that charge is expressly in the robbery. Section 18.2-192 of the code of Virginia names credit card larceny as a grand larceny (which is a lesser included of robbery). I basically told the court that by charging me for robbery and. red it card theft they convicted me for the same action twice. I made sure to point out that the only item the prosecution proved to be taken. Mr. Platania had a rebuttal but my mentioning of evidence presented cut that off. He then had the nerve to come out of his mouth and say, "I think there was evidence of other things that were in addition to the credit cards." I asked him to remind us what evidence besides credit cards being stolen. I got rebuked for speaking directly to the prosecution (I really didn't know it wasn't allowed). The judge admitted that it was a good point and that he couldn't remember.... Never found out because Mr. Platania interjected. Conveniently, no one had transcripts. Going back to the trial, she said that her credit cards were in a credit card wallet/phone case. Her wallet was in her book bag and she retained that. We know damn well they didn't show anything for the missing iPhone because they somehow forgot to look for it. They did not even attempt to prove that anything else was take. Let her tell it, I was kind enough not to take her laptop. Such a generous monster I am.

They rallied and shot me down. The judge referred to his notes, not the actual court record, and decided they were inbound. But I wasn't done. In my head anyway.

I brought up prosecution's knowing use of perjured testimony. By this time I know it is a waste of time but I had to proceed so that it would be there for later.

The thing about accusing them of knowingly using perjured testimony is that it goes beyond what they know into what they should know. They interview and reinterviewed witnesses. It was rehearsed before we met on the field of battle. Through all of that they take on the responsibility weeding out all lies an deceits. The Code of Virginia says that perjury by a witness must be supported by two other witnesses giving contradictory testimony. I mentioned two professional witnesses, whom the prosecution put on the stand, that described Naomi as calm and collected. Even another roommate, in her interview with the cops, said that she was surprisingly calm.

Well Jesse Dusk, another roommate and best friend, got on the stand and said that she wasn't. She said that she was panicked, distraught, distressed and terrified. I believe that she compared her to a deer or a squirrel frozen in horror. He allowed that such "might have" affected the jury. They tried to play it off as something small. The Supreme Court emphasized that "the jury's estimate of the truthfulness and reliability of a given witness may well be determinative of guilt or innocence." Factors as the possible interest of the witness in testifying falsely the defendant's life or liberty may depend.

I went on to tell the judge that "While it might be a small issue and, of course, the jury derived their own opinion of the situation, that small incident was enough, it have been enough..."

This ass looked at me and said "And you had a reason to testify falsely too, because your liberty was on the line. So both of you had a stake in this and the jury knew that." I should've been like "Fine, two penalties replay second down," but I was too... amazed by the openly one-sidedness of the hearing. I tried, and I played by the rules. I wasn't completely done just yet. There is something called a Petition for Writ of Error. This is one of the dinosaurs of legal forms but it is still applicable in Virginia. The problem is that very few judges or lawyers know anything about it. But ignorance is not an excuse to compromise someone's rights.

There are branches for a Writ of Error. There is Coram Nobis and Coram Vobis. Nobis is generally used to fix errors of the court after the sentence has been completed. Vobis allows you to bring the error before the court in which it occurred so that they can fix their own mistake.

According to the code of Virginia, when a person sentenced to imprisonment informs a court of their intent to file a Petition for a Writ of Error Coram Vobis, the judge is supposed to temporarily suspend execution of that sentence and grant enough time for said person to prepare and submit the petition. When I informed Judge Moore of my intent he said "Well, the writ of error is basically an appeal. We have a petition for appeal, you look for a writ of appeal."

I tried to explain the procedure of Coram Vobis Writ of Error.

His response, "I don't know anything about that." He looked at the prosecution, "Do you?"

The Truth, Yet I'm Not Free

Mr. Platania, always the type to be honest and play by the rules says, "No. That can be taken up on the direct appeal." He was wrong but he accidentally slipped a grain of truth in there.

I don't have the exact quote (Albemarle Charlottesville Regional Jail's law library was may helpful than anything DOC offers) but there is a case that says no court has the right to deny a person sentenced their right to file for a Petition for Writ of Error and that the act in itself is appealable. Its an extra challenge before proceeding up to the state court of appeals. An extra inning or overtime.

My current court appointed attorney refused to put it in the appeal that I was challenging the fact that the court denied me my chance to file for a Writ of Error. For a couple of reasons, I am not putting his name up as an enemy, whether he is or not... First, I don't think it was malicious. Very few attorneys understand the dynamics of this extraordinary writ because it is rarely used. He informed me that appeals have a size or volume limit and he felt that his points stood a better chance. Of course I disagreed but he was moving forward on what he thought was best. I still considered him an enemy but his paralegal (I will not name out of respect as well) took the time to stop and listen. That is something that very few criminal attorneys know how to do. Plus, I have all of my emails and my mother's emails and my sister's email to print out and attach to my Habeus Corpus.

The Truth, Yet I'm Not Free

Closing Argument

Some people who read this (I hope it's a lot) may wonder what I hoped to accomplish. After I was convicted, I attempted to get my story the same type of exposure I got when I was arrested. None of the newspapers would even give me a response.

I found my rock bottom at some point. I didn't want to be here anymore. I don't care about what people say and think until it reaches certain people I love. Their opinion matters. My mother, my sisters, a friend named Mallory, a friend named Jessica. It would hurt me to the soul if they believed this shit. I wanted out. I decided that my mothers and sisters could mourn for a few months and then they'll be okay as opposed to supporting me financially, emotionally, spiritually. They have been helping me with my damn research. I am a burden alive. Pain is constant while I am alive. Dead, it would be temporary. "It's guaranteed you gonna die, and you might be missed for maybe two or three hours, til they light their spliff." If it wasn't for a few good people at Nottoway Correctional Center, I wouldn't be here right now typing and still fighting. Lieutenant Whitehead took time to explain to me from personal experience the aftermath of suicide. Officer Bailey took time to make sure your mind is on positive stuff instead of the bad. She needs to stop bullshitting take that treatment officer post and save people. Escort Officer Wright knew how to listen.

This was real. I didn't slash my arm and show it. I didn't fake like I was hanging myself. I rigged my door up so it would be (I thought) impossible to get in, then I took a shit ton of pills of all sorts put my music in my ear, then laid down. I did make them get the camera though. Some people are really going through shit but there aren't many people that give a damn. I figured when they investigate my suicide they would expose those who needed exposing. Somehow Whitehead freed my door then I woke up in the hospital. With COVID. Now I'm medicated and drowning myself in my fiction writing. I won't taint this by advertising. FYI, this can be verified by contacting Nottoway Correctional Center

The Truth, Yet I'm Not Free

Three years later after September 19, 2018, I am putting the whole truth out for as cheap as I possibly can (Its free to read with Kindle Unlimited) so that it may cross the path of someone who can help me. Barring that, I really intend to start a nonprofit that will attack issues other people shy away from. By listing the names of all the corrupt fuc--- excuse me, individuals in the description then feeding it to the newspaper in their city, my hope is that it will spread faster. Once a story like this catches the right eye, the result that follows will be satisfactory in one way or another.

The best part, everything that I said is verifiable can be looked into using reference directory following my contact information. I read a quote somewhere but I can't remember where. "Start where you are. Use what you have. Do what you can." If you feel that you can help me in anyway, please contact me. Thank you for your time.

Jowell Le Gendre 1200238

Keen Mountain Correctional Center

P.O. Box 860

Oakwood, VA 24631

or

setup email on Jpay.com or with the Jpay app

my state number is #1200238

The Truth, Yet I'm Not Free

REFERENCE DIRECTORY

The first set was lumped together pages numbering from 1 to 841. It includes hearing for the following dates in this order.

6/17/19, 7/9/19, 7/17/19, 10/29/19, 11/6/19, 11/7/19, 11/8/19, 2/10/20(sentencing)

P.9-12, Ghost hearing

P. 13, Lines 21-25 Court asked if Ms. Vradenburgh's motion to withdraw came after my letter to her

P. 14, Lines 3-13 Ms. Pather saying we had a bench and a jury, Ms. Vrandenburgh telling them I was never arraigned and what they had were presets from Ms. Shepard (who is she?)

P. 15, Lines 1-14 Judge asked if I was requesting new counsel, I said no

P.16, Lines 1-6 Ms. Vradenburgh says that she didn't want to go through with the preliminary hearing because Ms. Pather asked her to think of the victim. She chose victim's comfort over my case

P.19, Lines 22-24 I choose objectives, attorney helps to define the means

P.20 Lines 7-10 Ms. Vradenburgh speak on our relationship as client and counsel

P.27 Lines 14-15 Judge contacted attorneys himself (proper?)

7/17/19 Hearing. Assigned Mr. Martin

P.34, Lines 6-9 Another attorney from Mr. Martin's office telling me that he was on vacation that week and the following week. Earliest he could have looked into my case was 8/1/19. Three months before trial.

P.36, Lines 2-5 Mr. Martin waited u til 10/25/19 to request expert witness trial set for 11/5/19

P.42, Lines 5-8 victim mentions nothing about sexual assault

P.52, Lines 11-13 Mr. Martin asking, at my request, that the record to show that I attempted to see evidence. it didn't

P.62-63 decided to arraign me then and there.

P.63, Lines 12-14 Martin doesn't explain the process, he just says plead not guilty

P.74, Lines 3-7 Telling judge I had no knowledge of video evidence until recently

P.99, Lines 20-22 Judge Moore skipping some sort of colloquy at the start of jury selection, violate due process?

P.100, Lines 11-13 in reference to P.99 admitting that he was still supposed to do whatever it was, cut corners violative of due process?

P.123, Lines 23-25 informs the court that he knows Commonwealth's Attorney Mr. Platania

P.128, Lines 3 judge mentions damaging info to jury

P.193, Line 17 Ms. Pather describes Naomi as hysterical

P.195, Lines 22-25, P.196 Lines 1-2 Ms. Pather says that Naomi was forced to perform oral sex with a bloody mouth but she wasn't raped because attacker had no condom

P.196, Lines 4-8 Ms. Pather says Naomi was told to get on the ground she refused because she feared being raped

P.198 Lines 7-8 Ms. Pather mentions my blood getting on the victim without saying how

T12

P.205, Line 3 Naomi lists the items in her bag

P.207, Lines 1-2 Naomi saying someone walked by her fast get she saw something concealed

P.208, Lines 17-20 Naomi describes herself during attack

P. 208, Line 25 she describes herself as hysterical

P.210, Lines 12-14 Naomi says she doesn't remember how she got to the back of the house

P.212 Lines 2-14 Describes the search of her book bag

P.214 Line 2, penetrated by an entire finger

P. 215 Describing how she was or wasn't on the ground

P.219, Lines 22-25 Tells roommate that she was robbed then asks for the phone to call cops

P. 220 Played 911 phone call. Went out as a robbery

P.220, Lines 18-19 Saying she told roommate she was sexually assaulted

P.222, Lines 9-12 Damage to front of mouth but attacked from the side

P.245, Lines8-12 Mr. Martin questioning her about direction of attack

P.246, Lines 5-8 cut on lip came from. punch or umbrella

P.247, Lines 21-25 Never fought back or injured me

P.250, Lines 20-25 repeating she never injured me

P.278, Lines 4-5 Detective Cole describes Naomi as solemn, calm, very objective

P.302, Lines 18-20 Detective Cole saw no injuries on me

P.321, Lines 17-21 No injuries

The Truth, Yet I'm Not Free

P.324, Lines 22-23 No injuries from elbow down

P.386, Lines 13-16 Response to defense's objection to text on paper (text still readable when jury is alone with evidence)

P.394, Lines 31-19 Lieutenant Newberry says he saw any wounds on unclothed body parts

P.396, Lines 4-7 Lt Newberry saying officers responded to robbery

P.476, Lines 17-18 Officer Waddy responded to a robbery call

P.483, Lines 1-4 Ms. Pather asked what kind of information Officer Waddy sought

P.484, Lines 8-9 Officer Waddy describing Naomi initial statement

P.484, Lines 14-24 after some time passes she amends story, no video

P.489, Lines 6-8 Officer Waddy asked her to "readvise" her story

P.492, Line 17 Detective Kim Hiner works property cases was assigned to rape scene

P.519, Lines 6-9 Wendy Travis example of paid time off

Sentencing

P.791, Lines 16-18 Telling me I'm pro se

p.792, Lines 11-14 Judge Moore justifying me not being represented

P.792, Line 20 and P.793, Lines 1-2 Judge Moore telling purpose of standby counsel

P.794, Line 22 Me letting the court know that I didn't understand

P.798-P.801 I asked for a chance to look at evidence my lawyer had

P.801, Lines 23-25 judge letting Commonwealth know their obligations with exculpatory evidence

The Truth, Yet I'm Not Free

P.802, Lines 20-22 I told judge evidence I requested would support motion

P.803, Lines 4-7 I told court attorney was refusing to use evidence he had in his possession

P.804, Lines 4-7 preserving all motions and exceptions for appeals

P.806-813 Me arguing double jeopardy clause

P.810, Line 12-14 Blatant lie by Commonwealth

P.811 He says phone and wallet, she said "card wallet", the other was in her bag

P.814-820 Me arguing prosecution knowingly using perjured testimony

P.822, Line 25 Me telling court that I did not receive presentence report in the required 5 day time space

P.823-824, Commonwealth allowed to make extensive record

The next three hearings came separately

10/3/19 Hearing

P.3, Lines 21-22 Mr. Martin informs the Court that I don't trust him

P.4, Lines 2-3

Mr. Martin tells court I have no faith in his abilities

*Continued bench trail 30 days to prepare for trial

P.6, Lines 15-18 Manipulating Ms. Vradenburgh's withdrawal

P.6, Lines 22-25 Deliberately lying about attorneys withdrawing and changing my reasons for needing new counsel

P.7 Commonwealth and judge put witness comfort before my rights

The Truth, Yet I'm Not Free

P.8, Lines 22-25 Mr. Martin refused to show letter from Vradenburgh

P.11, Lines5-9 putting on record Mr. Martin refusing to show evidence I had on hand about Ms. Vradenburgh

1/28/20 Hearing

P.5, Line 25 I inform court it was Ms. Vradenburgh's request

P.6 Me trying explain I want counsel Mr. Martin removed but I'm not requesting his removal

P.8, Lines 19-22 Commonwealth clearly manipulating of July 9, 2019

P.9, Line 8 I tried to correct Commonwealth, judge aggressively forbid it

P.19, Lines 8-9 I'm officially pro se

P.21-27 Setting the record straight about attorneys

P.28 Lines 3-4 I try to point out neither of my first 2 attorneys complained about my personality, judge became hostile

P.29, Lines 6-8 judge giving his reason to deny me counsel

P.29, Lines 19-20 the why doesn't matter to judge

P.31, Line 20 judge refused to see evidence supporting motions

P.32, Line 24 and P.33, Line 1-2 nothing in motion would be basis for mistrial

P.34 judge ignoring case law about ineffective assistance counsel

P. 36, Lines 4-7 Hobson's Choice

P.41, Lines 10-13 denying me help with paperwork and research for motions

The Truth, Yet I'm Not Free

2/10/20 Probation Violation

P.4, Lines 23-24 I informed court I have not seen violation report

P.5, Lines 10-16 Informing court of intent to file Writ of Error

P.6, Lines 5-8 Me explaining writ

P.6, Lines 9-24 and P.7 Lines 1-8 court denying me right to file petition for writ of error

www.ingramcontent.com/pod-product-compliance
Lightning Source LLC
Chambersburg PA
CBHW060901260726
48661CB00008B/3382